This book is dedicated to my grandparents

Pablo y Julia

Thank you for teaching me about business

I know you are in Heaven smiling down at me

Table of Contents

About the Author

I think I was born to be a Realtor. Well, maybe. Here is my story.

When I was a little girl, my grandparents owned three fully paid houses on a lot. No mortgage. They drilled the fact into me that when they died, the homes would belong to me. Year after year passed, and they continued to assure me they were leaving me the three houses. I will never forget the day my grandmother died. I was rushed to see her in the hospital, but she was no longer coherent. My grandfather was devastated. So was I. I would visit my grandfather as much as possible, and during those visits, he would remind me that the homes were mine and not to forget that.

You see, the reason why they wanted to make sure I knew this was because of my dad, a Vietnam Veteran. He came back from the

Vietnam War with PTSD. He was a mess. He turned to drugs and a life of crime. My grandparents did not want to lose everything they worked so hard for.

The day my grandfather died was hell. You can read about that story in my memoir, "WAR DAD" by Juju Sands. After some time had passed, my dad and I went to an attorney for the reading of the Will. When the attorney refused to speak to me, I was confused. I was advised that the Will had been changed and my dad was now in charge. How could that be? Well, my dad coerced my grandfather to take me out of the Will. I will never know the true story behind that, but, facts were facts, and I was out. My dad was not in his right mind. I knew I had to help him or we would lose everything. One day, I got a call from my grandparents neighbor. She told me to get there right away because the houses were on fire. All 3 of them. It was too late, though. By the time I got there, it was all burnt to the ground, ashes everywhere. My dad was nowhere to be found.

I will never forget that day; I felt ripped off. There went my college fund. There went my head-start in life. There went everything for which my grandparents worked so hard. I wanted to throw up. I drove away, and could not look back. I had lost everything my grandparents left me. Everything I owned. This was my first huge blow in life, and I was only 18. To attempt to get control of my emotions and keep from losing my mind, I told myself that I would start over. I would build my own wealth. I would buy my own home.

That day, I asked God to help me get through. I needed to rely on my faith. I promised myself that I would be successful in life; no matter what. It became my mission to own three homes. That was how my affair with real estate began. By the way, it still hurts....

Be the kind of woman
Who wakes up every morning
and accepts nothing less
from herself
than to give her
all

Julie Sands

I Am Not Sane, I Am Just Saying

Often, some stay-at-home moms or ladies perhaps just like you, who are looking for an easy career to get into, jump into real estate. Now, you may be facing the reality that it is not quite as easy as they make it look on TV or as the person who recruited you said it was going to be. There is a lot of work involved. There are several key components to becoming a successful real estate Agent. There are also some secrets and tips that top producers practice to earn top dollar.

I never had anyone lay out a plan for me. I learned from trial and error; from mistakes and successes and a lot of prayers to get me through. I developed a system that works for me. When I needed to revamp or adjust my tactics, I did. In this book, I will share some of those tools with you to help you generate the money that you have set out to make. You will learn how to market yourself, and know what to say to people. I will also teach you how to practice role-playing to get comfortable with your lines of script, so you will become powerful and efficient in what you do. I will give you raw advice and steps to take as well as golden nuggets of inside information on how many successful women live their days.

If you stick with me through this book, I promise that by the time you are finished reading, you will have new skills that will help you get that listing and effectively start the journey to become the top real estate agent in your community. I have been called an extremist, a person who thinks out-of-the-box, and more. I have had to put those opinions aside and live in my power; what I know to be right. Some of it may be too much to handle, but I advise you to try. So, if you're ready, let us do it.

LET'S DIVE IN!

Just Trust Me On This One

This was my scenario. I was a young mom, raising two kids, trying to keep a clean house and get dinner on the table, every day. I was a team mom, room mom, PTA member and a lunchtime proctor at my daughter's school. In all this craziness, I still wanted a career. I had to find a way to fit that career in and keep my kids and husband as my priority.

This book is a quick review of my experience and the experience of other successful women Realtors. There is so much more I could share, but I would have produced a 400-page book, and honestly, I don't have time to write 400 pages. LOL! I recommend getting a business coach. Invest in yourself and learn from the pros.

Before you decide you want a career that will take up more time than you think it will, make sure the following are clean and organized. Just trust me on this one.

Organize your:
- Home and closets
- Cars – they must be clean and free of trash
- Desk or cubicle
- Front yard or porch
- Backyard or balcony
- Pantry or kitchen cabinets
- Refrigerator and freezer
- Laundry room

You cannot be unorganized and be successful! When you are organized, you can find things. In addition to being organized, you must live and work in a clean environment. For me, when my house is not clean, I cannot function. When my bed is left unmade, or there are dishes in the sink, I feel as if there is a monkey on my back. However, when I am on schedule, following my to-do list, and my house is clean and organized, I can concentrate on work because my mind is free of cluttered thoughts, and I just feel better.

Many women hire a cleaning service. That is something I can probably incorporate into my life; I just have not had time to do that. So, I do it myself. I will show you my list, and it might be a little overwhelming for you. Nevertheless, it is how I live.

Once a week:
- Bathrooms
- Kitchen wipe-down, kitchen stove and clean out fridge
- Dust
- Sweep or vacuum, mop
- Wash clothes, wash cars

Take a look at your
DEBT

Take a look at your
DREAMS

Take a look at your
CIRCUMSTANCES

**NOW TELL ME IF YOU CAN
PROCRASTINATE
ANOTHER DAY**

Julie Sands

A Thousand Doors

I am currently a top-producing Realtor. I have attained a very desirable status at a high-end real estate company. When I first started selling real estate, I was part of a team. Our leader and top producer sold a lot of homes, but she was not very nice to work with. So, even though I was making some money, I felt unfulfilled. I didn't feel that it was worth it, so I left that team and went on my own. However, I began facing the harsh reality that going on my own meant that I needed to start from scratch. I was terrified because I didn't have any leads or any listings; it was just me.

My broker told me that she would give me 500 black and white copies a month, and that was pretty much all I had to market myself, get listings and be successful. I decided to set a goal. I was going to knock on a thousand doors every month. Now, how am I going to turn those 500 copies into 1,000 so that I could hand something to every single one of those doors that I knocked on? I took each sheet of paper, divided it in half, and made half page postcards for each page. Of course, I had to cut each one of them individually. For the next three months, I handed out 1,000 fliers each month. I spoke to people in the supermarket, in parking lots, and in elevators. Everywhere I went, I talked to people about their real estate needs. Understand that you are going to talk more than you have probably ever talked in your whole life to be successful.

Yes, I Got Caught

Work on building a reputation as the 'go-to person' in your community, and then continue promoting yourself and making yourself visible. Wear your badge everywhere you go and talk to people; don't just put your face on signs. When you are having a conversation, you will never know who is going to be the person that will award you a listing. All this effort comes together at some point and allows you the opportunity to sit down with somebody at their house and talk to them about listing their house with you. You need to be ready for this! Be overly prepared when you arrive at the Seller's house because it all starts before you ever get there. It begins with your research. Understand the market you are in and the value of the houses in the area. It is more than just pulling the comps; you need to know what those comps are saying and understand the plusses and minuses of that person's house so you can talk about them in detail. But you, as a Realtor, also need to be prepared to speak to this client.

I remember my very first open house. An attorney arrived and began questioning me in a patronizing manner. He could tell I was a newer Agent. I am not sure if he was trying to bully me or if he was just simply enjoying pushing me to see how knowledgeable I was. I remember getting flustered and stumbling on my words. What I learned from that situation was the importance of knowing what you are talking about. It is not something you can fake. You need to know your stuff; the numbers, the competition, the area and more. Have every piece of information about the house you are listing and then selling, down cold. It is time for you to embrace being ready and fully prepared because when that first listing call comes in, that person will be looking to trust you with selling their house. Always remember that even one person who does a listing with you can be worth up to $6,000 plus in commission. Yes, from just that one person.

Seeing The big Picture

Marketing yourself isn't always easy. In fact, being a Realtor is not as easy as I thought. You have probably run into that truth yourself. I remember after knocking on those first five hundred doors, meeting dogs, being chased by dogs, being followed, being whistled and honked at; and still not receiving any phone calls. I was so discouraged!

I wish I could tell you that a hundred people out of those first one thousand fliers listed homes with me and that I made a million dollars in my first three months. But I did not. I was not even sure if any of those people were among my first listings. My first listing is not clear to me. What is clear, is how I consistently knocked on those doors. It would have been easy to have stepped away from real estate and looked for another career, but I always had confidence. I knew that what I was doing was creating a 'buzz' about me. Eventually, I became part of the community and earned my reputation as the 'expert in real estate.'

You know that it is starting to happen when people start referring to you as 'The Real Estate Lady.' In fact, I realized the other day when somebody mentioned, "There's the real estate lady," in the parking lot, that it was a title I not only gladly wore, but it was something I was never going to lose.

You will be well served to learn to see the big picture. Do not lose focus on what is in front of you because of what singular action that you need to take at that moment. I encourage you to be confident because your hard work will pay off if you don't give up.

Posture, Lipstick, Nails And Hair

One of the things that I always talk about with the people I coach is the importance of their posture and overall appearance. Preparing your image is something you'll want to do before you walk into the client's house to talk to them about listing with you. Your presentation and image is something you should have cared about from the moment you started handing out your first flier, and it needs to continue all the way through your career.

I cannot stress enough how important it is that you always look presentable because unfortunately, no one in your office is probably brave enough to walk up to you and tell you that you need to clean up to be successful. There is an image people expect from you and an image that you want to uphold.

Let us talk about successful people, and start with successful Realtors. You cannot deny the fact that they have 'presentation.' Have you noticed what happens when successful people walk into a room? They instantly radiate wealth, knowledge, and success. How about the top producers in your office? Have you noticed their gestures, manner of speaking and how straight they stand? It's because they are confident, they know their stuff, they command respect and your full attention. Even if you do not want to give it, it just happens. Aside from their posture, they smell good and dress nicely too. Now, let's talk about the people who are the complete opposite. Have you ever wanted to approach someone and they just don't feel approachable? Perhaps they don't make eye contact, or they are hard to read. If you ask me, I would prefer dealing with someone who stands tall, looks and smells good, rather than deal with someone who slouches, doesn't make eye contact, and has a piece of lettuce in their teeth. Make an impression that will make people comfortable and proud to hire you.

I will never forget the day I walked into an open house and walked right by the Listing Agent. The picture on the sign did not look like the person inside the house. In the photo, her hair was nicely styled, her make-up looked great, and she was wearing a very nice dress. She looked professional, and that was what I was expecting to see. As I walked into the house, I noticed a lady holding a notepad, but she did not look like the lady on the sign. Her hair was not groomed, her mascara was all over the place, she smelled like cigarettes, and her outfit was not the most professional. I did not recognize her. I visited a few more of her open houses, and she was always the same. She once had red lipstick way, way, way outside of the lines of her lips………. LOL! On a serious note, I understand that we all come from different backgrounds, and we all have different styles, but that is not what I am addressing here. What I am talking about is professionalism; looking like a well-groomed, well-rounded and strong Realtor that your clients can be proud of. Personally, I find that when I am "put together," I feel better. And when I feel better, I can produce better.

Another important thing that can help is to find somebody in your office that you can model after. Let me tell you about a Realtor in my office that I look up to. She has short blonde hair and it's styled nicely every day. Her nails are always done, makeup is always on point, and she always smells great. She always dresses to impress. She knows how to carry herself and how to uphold that image. She knows how to separate herself from all the ordinary and average agents. She knows how to be the person that you can trust to list your house, sell it, and get you the maximum value for it. Like a normal Realtor, she started at the bottom and worked her way up. She has been in the industry for over 30 years and has been a consistent Top Producer. Another reason I love her is that she is positive and knowledgeable about the business. When she speaks, I listen. Now, she has millionaire clients, and I assume she is a millionaire as well.

When you uphold a good image of yourself, you separate yourself from the ordinary. When you look good, you feel good, and you gain self-confidence. Your clients and others can feel that self-confidence, and it helps them to trust you. This is critical in our industry. Your clients and potential clients must feel they can trust you within the first minute of speaking with you. Successful Realtor's strive to look good all the time; even when we do not feel like it.

Listing

You can be a Listing Agent, a Buyer's Agent, or both, but the Listing Agent is more in control of the transaction. The key is to be good enough to get the listing. Remember that the seller is looking to sell the property for the highest dollar amount possible, and that is why the seller needs an Agent who is extremely knowledgeable in market value for the area and in selecting quality buyers.

Be prepared for your listing presentation with the following:

1. Your listing presentation.
Have your comps and your proposal printed out in color. Color copies make houses look more impressive and allow the person to see both advantages and disadvantages of their house as compared to the other homes currently on the market. There is nothing less

memorable than an Agent showing comparable houses in the neighborhood to a prospective client, with pictures in black and white. People need that visual to help them. If you are serious about your career, you want your presentation to look serious; not like something that you just printed right before you walked out the door of your office. Keep all your materials in high quality.

2. A copy of the Property profile from your Title company.

3. Market trends for the area.

4. Listing Agreement and Seller disclosures.

5. Timeline of procedures.

6. A list of benefits, and what you will do for the Seller that sets you apart.

Developing a Connection

Your first goal as the client answers their door for a listing appointment is to begin building rapport. Developing a connection with your potential future seller is essential. Why? We all buy from people who we know, like, and trust. That connection starts immediately from the moment they meet you. If you give them a bad first impression, it will be tough for you to overcome the hurdle of a person not feeling you are trustworthy. Remember: Relationships are key, and you must connect with your potential client on their level.

As you walk into the house, be observant. Listen to the story the house is telling you because every house has one. I normally look around discreetly to see if I can find something to use as a conversation anchor. Are there a lot of family photos on display? Are there people or pets in these photos that I could talk to them about? You need to get to know them on a personal level. Give them the perfect opportunity to see you as someone who's genuine.

If the personality of the house isn't clear, I fish around for clues in the house to talk about. I find the hot point that shows off what the owners are proud of and what they're into. From there, it's easy to lead them into talking about those subjects. Get comfortable with them. Get familiar with one other, and soon you will discover that you are creating long-term relationships.

Remember, it is your responsibility to connect with the Seller. After all, they are considering you for one of the largest financial transactions they will ever experience, so they need to feel comfortable with you. Part of this relationship building is in creating a sense that you are all a part of a team; you're not just somebody who is invading their home. Sometimes, this means spending enough time to get comfortable with the lady of the house before you even start talking about their home. You'll want to get her on board with your ideas. Later, you will be staging the house, and if you haven't created a good rapport with her, I guarantee, you will have a challenge. Making suggestions regarding how a home should be changed is always a sensitive subject. So, put aside your ego, humble yourself, and figure out a way to connect - especially with the wife.

Taking the Tour

IMPORTANT: Write things down!

Do not forget to take down notes while taking a tour of the house. Don't expect to remember everything; whether it is details about the house or the family. Write everything down because you will need to refer to this information later.

Now, we can take the tour.

As a Listing Agent, know what you are getting yourself into. Integrity is key to having a long career. You have a name and a reputation. So too, the seller has a name and things that are important to them. Remember your reputation as you walk through the house because your picture is going to be out front on the sign. That picture tells the whole world, 'this is the *kind of house that this Agent is going to show and possibly sell to me.'*

Even though my seller is eager to hear where I am planning to price their home, I make them wait, and here's why: **I cannot place a value on a home without knowing the inner workings of the house.**

It's much like first meeting a new person. You can't understand their full value or be totally yourself because you don't know them yet. Once you have gotten to know them, then you can decipher how much of yourself you will give. Right? It's the same with a house. You cannot give it a true dollar value until you become familiar with the entire house.

As you tour the house, put all your senses into action.

What do you see?

Are there cracks in the walls? Are there foundation issues? How is the flooring or carpet? Will it need cleaning or replacing? Is there a problem with the paint or is there a funky paint color? Are the windows new or do they look old and worn? Is the roof in good shape? Does the house look clean? Is there clutter?

What do you smell?

I once went into a home that smelled musty. I could not put my finger on it, so I kept inquiring. I asked them, *"Have you ever had a mold problem?"* and they said, *"No, I do not think we ever have."* As I was walking through the house, I finally found it in the bathroom of the master's bedroom; a probable mold problem that needed to be addressed. The shower tiles were missing grout, the water was seeping into the walls as they showered, and the result was a musty smell. I needed to be up front with them and advised them that it needed to be taken care of. A buyer will notice these things, and remember, it is your name and face on the sign. Always act with the utmost integrity and ensure that the buyer is getting a safe home to the best of your ability. It is your job as the real estate professional, to be the first one to bring up issues like the mold problem I just referred to.

What do you hear?

I love selling older homes and period homes. I have sold homes that were built in 1901, all the way up to homes built in 1925. I have learned to listen to noises, because some may have further meaning.

Take this old two-story home that I had toured. I remembered hearing squeaking noises as I walked up the stairs. Most do, so I was not too worried about it. That all changed when I got into one of the bedrooms. The floor squeaked as I walked in and there was a spot that felt loose. The first thing I thought about was termite damage. I asked the seller to order a termite inspection right away. Your job is to make that house appealing to a buyer. The buyer must be able to see themselves living in that house. It's better to allow your seller to know the truth and fix it, as opposed to a nasty surprise when you are in escrow. At that point, you are trying to put out a fire, and the best way to avoid fires in real estate is not to let them start.

It is your job to get top dollar for your Seller.

Along with your list of "fixes" you want a complete list of upgrades the seller has made. List them all; none are too small. Improvements are important to the seller, and they are always proud of their upgrades. Many times, you will factor the upgrades into the value of the house.

As you are touring, ask questions about the history of the home. This includes any second loans or lines of credit the seller has on the title of that house. The more you know, the better you can serve your client and preserve your integrity.

Pricing the House

Now it is time to sit down and talk numbers.

As a Realtor, you are expected to know your stuff. When the seller asks you something, and you don't know the answer, never say, *"I don't know."* Instead, say: *"I will find out and get back to you."*

You will factor upgrades to the home as they compare to other properties in the area as well as repairs that will be completed before the house goes on the market as you compute your listing price. Sometimes, a person can make a larger profit with a small upgrade, but the buyer needs to be aware of those upgrades. Inform your seller of all the problems and potential problems with the house. Don't try to hide them. I guarantee you when the buyer comes through; they are going to be looking at every single detail. It doesn't reflect well on you when the buyer is the one who points out a problem to the seller.

As the Realtor, you are expected to have the ability to spit out a listing price on the fly. You'll be expected to be able to calculate all this information on the spot. This is why I am coaching you to know your market like the back of your hand. Know the models, square footage, neighborhood, and know what has sold, went pending, expired, and so on for the last three years.

Once you have discussed a price with the seller, it is time to sign the listing agreement. Always give the seller a timeline of the listing process, the escrow process, and the closing process. This will leave all the guessing out, and they will know that you have control of the situation.

Note: *If you feel you need help in this area or any area of being a successful Realtor, I recommend my coaching program. I had many coaches to help me succeed.*

Contracts

Successful Realtors know contracts. We have them memorized. We can even fill them out in our sleep. The worst thing you could do to in service to your client is not knowing your contracts and disclosures.

Every state has different contracts, and because of that, this chapter will be short. All I can tell you is that you had better know those contract and disclosures line by line. Yes, each line, each section and each page. You are hired to represent either a seller or a buyer. You are expected to know your stuff because you are being hired to be the expert in real estate.

Keep in mind that if a legal issue were to arise about something in those contracts, you would have big problems on your hands. It is better to avoid that. Make sure you know your contracts and that you understand every word of them. If you need further help, contact your local association because they may have classes. You can also talk to your Broker and find out if they can go over each contract with you.

Staging

For me, staging is the most exciting part of my job.

Staging is the act of preparing the house that is to be sold so that it is positioned to compete against other homes in the area. In my world, I like my homes to be above the competition!

Staging ensures the entire home is organized and de-cluttered.

Staging increases the possibilities of a faster sale.

Staging will help get the seller the asking price or come close.

Staging makes you think like a buyer.

I know many Agents who hire staging companies to come in and stage the homes for them. If your seller has the funds to do that, why not do it? I always try to save my seller money in any way I can. Because of that, I always stage myself at no charge to my seller. It is one of the benefits they get when listing with me. I use what the seller has available.

Staging starts by hiring a cleaning crew. In real estate, you come across various styles of housekeeping. What is dirty to some might simply be a little dusty for others. What is unorganized to some might be just look like someone with a "busy schedule" to others. Since every client will live differently, you must have your own staging techniques and a fail-proof system. Remember, you are walking into your client's life. You are not a family member, and you cannot tell someone they live in a compromised way. Be gentle when coaching your client into staging. Keep in mind that the goal in staging is to provide an "I can see myself living here" environment for the buyers.

Successful Realtors are proud of their listings. When we put our sign in your front yard, it is as if we are standing there, 24/7 advertising our expertise. Taking pride in your listings is important. They are your social media and real-time advertisement, and they leave a footprint of your work.

Let's go, room by room.

After cleaning and de-cluttering the house, go room by room, and stage. Most of the time, the entire house will have white walls. If the walls are multi-colored, a paint job might be inevitable. If the walls in the house are all one color, just make sure they are clean. There are times when your seller cannot afford to hire a painter, or they just do not want to paint. In this case, I encourage you to work with what you have.

Let us start with the living room. Whatever room the buyer walks into first, must be welcoming. Usually, it is the living room or the family room. Families spend a lot of time in those rooms. If they have children, or plan to, the living room and family room are even more important in the choice of a home. The family room will also serve as an entertainment space. Regardless of the size of these two rooms, they should look bright, airy and clean. They must smell good and have live plants to give them a touch of elegance. Remove all family pictures and replace them with generic ones. The buyers need to envision themselves there, not your sellers' family. As for the furniture, arrange it in a way that is communal or conversational, yet maximizes the space. If the couches are worn, consider slipcovers or decorative throws. If the flooring is not too nice, a big area rug with some red color is always good. I like to incorporate accents of red because it is a powerful color and it's pleasing to the eye.

Now, let us go to the kitchen.

The kitchen is a huge selling point. You will want to highlight space. The windows should be clean and have clean window coverings. Stainless steel appliances should be sparkling. Cabinet faces should be clean. Counter space is money; make sure they are clear and free of daily appliances. Instead, buy fresh, small, green, house plants in red vases and stage those on the counters. NEVER have old fruit sitting on the counters. I once walked into a kitchen with old bananas on a platter with gnats flying everywhere. That killed the warm fuzzy feeling of my buyer. Everything should feel fresh and clean. If a plug-in air scent is needed, by all means, buy one for every room.

Now, let us proceed to the bedroom. Bedrooms are sacred spaces and hold the scent of the family living there — especially the kids' rooms. This is where your buyer will either like the home or not. I have seen buyers love the entire home but abruptly change their minds after they see the master bedroom. Keep in mind that all the bedrooms must look spacious, comfortable and clutter free. The walls must be in a decorative staged form; not too much on them. All things that pertain to the sellers personality should be removed. Invest in a new bedspread. Spiff up the curtains. Polish the furniture. Get a live palm tree in a vase and stage it in a corner. Depending on the sellers' budget, if new bedding is not an option, make sure you instruct the seller to wash all linen fabrics, shampoo all the carpets, and clean the windows including the window sills. Spiff up the bedrooms as much as possible. Do you get the picture? Clean, de-clutter, comfort, space, scent and welcoming are your target words. Oh, and do not forget the red accents and live plants.

Let us move outside.

Houses need curb appeal. It is the only way it can compete with the other houses on the market at first glance or with a drive-by. Grass must be green and manicured. Bushes must be trimmed. Clutter or junk must be removed. It must have a fresh look. Try planting flowers, install sod, plant some trees, or prune overgrown trees, and lay some bark or rock. Any spaces that have plain dirt must be staged.

The backyard is a family's oasis. This is where they make memories. It is where their children will play. It is where birthday parties, anniversaries, holidays and summers will be spent. It must be clutter-free, as spacious as possible, clean, and manicured. Stage it with new patio furniture.

I once staged a home that had grass and dirt patches that led to the back yard. I had to stage on a budget, so I raked the dirt, leveled it off, and had the Seller water it every night (yes, water the dirt). They had about five stone turtles that were supposed to be yard décor but were not being used. I cleaned them off and placed the family of turtles in a line in the dirt as if they were going into the back yard. It actually looked cute. You can also add new plants, new bark, new rock or whatever you see fit; just stage it! Look at magazines so you can learn how to stage a yard. The back yard should tell the buyer, *"I am good enough for you to bring your friends and family to."* Educate yourself and be creative, because your seller is counting on you to sell their house for top dollar. Let me say it again; you are supposed to be the expert.

A couple of years ago, I was selling a home with a pool in the back yard. The kids had left for college, and the parents never went into the backyard. It was overgrown and filled with junk. I must admit; I was a little overwhelmed. How was I going to get my seller to purge? It was going to be too much work for them. I could just hear the husband say, "We are selling as-is!" I knew that I could not list the home in that condition. My face and name will be on the yard sign. What type of reputation will this give me if I allow my seller to hit the market in bad shape? I had to have a heart to heart talk with the hubby. I decided to take him for a ride (not that kind of ride...lol) to see the other homes for sale in the neighborhood. As we walked into the back yards, they looked inviting, peaceful, fun, and clean. Then, I took him to see the higher priced homes that were for sale. We saw yards that made us feel like we were on vacation. When we got back to his home, I walked him into his backyard. The next day, he ordered a large commercial trash bin. The house sold in one open house, full price, cash offer for over $620K. When you work big, you earn big. You see, staging has been one of the biggest keys to my success. Well, staging, and the color Red!

Marketing Madness

Successful Realtors are always in marketing mode. We talk to everyone. We wear our badge, and our cars have a car magnet with our picture and phone number. We know that marketing never ends. We constantly look for ways to market ourselves. Nothing is out of the question. We think out of the box, and we can get radical.

We are so blessed in the current day and age we live in, to have social media as a marketing platform. Back in the day, marketing was something you did on foot, on the phone, or in print. Marketing is the key to your longevity, and that is why a successful Realtor never stops marketing. If you cannot afford to purchase marketing tools or products, get creative. Develop a marketing system that includes different styles and genres of marketing.

Social media

The key with social media is to interact. Successful Realtors use Social Media — in all forms like:

- Zillow featured agent
- Trulia featured agent
- Realtor.com featured agent
- Facebook, Instagram, Twitter, SnapChat, Pinterest
- And more

When you have a listing, buy a Facebook Ad or an Instagram Ad. Show your listing on all your social media pages. Send your listings to friends via social media. Post your listings on other sites. Don't just exclusively use social media. When you exclude other marketing avenues, you leave out all the people who do not use social media, and your local farm area.

Email

Whenever you hold an open house, collect email addresses during the open house, but don't stop there. Send emails to that list once a month or every other month. You can set up pre-scheduled emails to automate the process.

Door-to-door farming

Once you have chosen a farm area, you should visit your farm at least every other month. When I first started farming, I knocked on the doors of 1,000 homes a month. I know, that's a lot, but I was determined to succeed. These are the actions of a successful Realtor. We take on more than the normal.

To make my marketing easier, I have campaigns scheduled every month of the year. For example, in February, I may design a 3x5 postcard on glossy card stock. On one side, it would have my picture and information along with some local real estate news and the latest sale in my area. On the other side, it would have a "Valentine" themed story, poem, a good dinner recipe, or any other ideas for Valentine's Day. That postcard would be mailed to my contact list—also known as my "sphere." I can do a digital version also, and of course, emails take little to no money to send. The door-to-door farming/marketing, on the other hand, was a good way to stay in shape and meet people. After all, we are in the people business, right? So once you develop a full year's campaign, you can recycle the ideas and update as you go, but at least you have a system.

Networking

Networking can be as small as wearing your badge as you shop for groceries and talking to people while picking out fruit, or it can be as expansive as going to your company's convention and meeting other Agents. Successful Realtors are always in motion. You might think about joining a real estate networking group, or your local and national Realtors Association or other groups that allow you to advertise your services. Get involved with your community and volunteer. Most of the time, if you have done your job right, they will think of you when it comes to real estate services.

I personally use social media to network. I am in communication daily with other Realtors, my clients, and the public. Do not be afraid to post. Don't be scared to come out of your shell. There is a client out there who needs you, your personality, your knowledge and your care. There are so many ways to market yourself, and too many to mention in this short read. If you want to get more elaborate in your marketing, you can always start a blog and dive deeper into creating your personal brand.

Note: *If you feel you need help in this area or any area of being a successful Realtor, I recommend my coaching program. I will teach you proven techniques to marketing to make money.*

Open Houses

Successful Realtors hate doing open houses. LOL! It's true, but let's not go there.

THE TRUTH IS

Open houses can generate so many leads you won't know what to do with all of them. I have sold my listings from just one open house. The secret is knowing how to hold a proper open house to maximize the exposure you will get. When I was just starting, I did not have any listings, so I volunteered to do open houses for top producing Agents in the office. Of course, I did not like giving up my weekends, but I was determined to make a lot of money in real estate, and I needed clients to do that.

You will find that some clients do not like people in their homes, and I get that. If the home is in a compromised or rough area, I would not have an open house. It is just not worth it. Think of other ideas to sell the house. On the other hand, if your client is fine with an open house and it is in a safe area, it is a great way to draw people to your listing. Be sure to have a second pair of eyes to help you with security.

NEVER DO AN OPEN HOUSE ALONE

I had a situation where a homeless man followed my signs on foot and walked into the house while I was in the kitchen (which was at the back of the house). When I saw him, I immediately knew something was not right. I began to regret that I didn't sign up for that boxing class when I was ten years old. LOL! I did not know Kung Fu, nor did I have pepper spray, so I was feeling vulnerable. All I had were my teeth and my acrylic nails as my defense. I clearly had not put myself in a good position. As we made small talk, I walked my way to the front door and stood on the porch until he left. I could have been assaulted. The worst part is that I knew better. I once had a squatter pop out of a closet too…. But that's another story. LOL!

Let's assume you have successfully staged the house and it is spotless, de-cluttered and smells good. You are ready to do an open house and will want to get the word out. One way to do that is by creating a postcard or flyer that you can also use online. Along with the house information, the postcard should have the time and date of the open house. Another way is to send your flyer to your sphere via e-mail. Some other ways are advertising online, walking your flyer to the surrounding homes, taking out an ad in the local paper, informing local Realtors, or going to the local churches and passing out your flyers. Always think out of the box. Go onto social media and buy ads for your area. They are as cheap as $5.00 at times. No avenue is off limits.

On the day of your open house, make sure that you've planned everything ahead of time.

Where will you place your signs safely?
Will you serve refreshments?
Will you need fresh flowers?
Will you have candles or air scents?

Always have a couple of blank purchase agreements and a notepad so you can take new email addresses. Today is your day to shine. Today you get to advertise yourself to the public. Do not forget to place your signs strategically. Place them on busy street corners for free advertisement. As the signs get closer to the house, you can add balloons to your signs to create excitement. I always ask my seller to leave the house while I am holding the open house. This way, the cars are removed from the driveway, and you can peacefully work your magic with the potential buyers.

All windows and blinds should be opened unless there is an ugly view that you do not want to show.

Create a light and fresh atmosphere. Turn on every light in the house. Play smooth jazz softly in the background as it adds an air of elegance. You want to create a dream home for that buyer to enter. Follow guests that visit the home, and have your helper do the same. Be in motion; ask questions. Find out where those buyers are in their search for a new home. Always ask for an Agent's card if any of the guests arrive with one, so you can ask for feedback after your open house. Always do the follow up on the same day. If you got leads, they are hot, and you want to make a connection while they still remember you. Lastly, ensure your lipstick is within your lip lines. LOL!

Wearing Multiple Hats

As a Listing Agent, it is important that you understand your role. At times, you will wear more than one hat, such as counselor, house cleaner, or interior decorator. You will become intimately and intricately a part of a family during a very special time of their life; therefore, it is important for you to catch everything. You are supposed to be the expert, so be the expert. If you thought you were just showing up to sell a house, brace yourself, because it is much more than that. You are walking straight into the lives of your clients. You are becoming an important component in the biggest financial decision of their life. You are joining what may be the most emotional state you would every see someone in. Did you know that the emotions that come along with buying or selling of a house are equal to the emotions felt during a divorce? Yup. We work in a high emotion industry and guess what; you are the Realtor, so everything is YOUR fault. LOL!

I remember walking up to the door of a house that I was going to list. Before I could even get past the doorway, I could feel that the wife was resistant to list her house. I found out quickly that they were selling the house because they were getting divorced after 43 years of marriage. She didn't want the divorce and didn't want to sell the house; the husband did. It was a very tough situation for me to be in. I was uncomfortable and felt bad for the wife. She was crying and very upset. We spoke for an hour about how they got to this place. I was trying to counsel them into reconciliation, but the husband did not want to reconcile, so I slapped him. Just kidding! Each time you get a listing, as you prepare to meet those clients, you are stepping right into their life. There may be some unexpected areas that you become involved with. In the end, I was able to mediate the sale. I did not take sides. I simply kept them focused on the task at hand. When they would begin to argue in front of me, I would remind them of the outcome and how they needed to stay focused. In doing that, I could help them list and sell their house. If you are not prepared to handle a variety of emotional situations, if you do not understand up front the multiple hats that you may need to wear during the time that you are listing the house, it is going to be difficult for you to be the professional that this business requires.

I will never forget the 90-year-old client I worked with. She had lived in her house her whole life. She raised her children and lost her husband in that house. Needless to say, she was attached to the house. After I got the listing, I knew the next issue that needed to be tackled would be a deep clean. Years of memories were stored in that house, so I knew this was something that needed to be approached very gently. First, I asked her children to help declutter the house, but after two hours, she kicked them out of the house. The children called me and said, *"Mom will not let us declutter her house."* There were a lot of things that she just could not get rid of so I had to step in and help her. I arrived with boxes and cleaning supplies, and I said to her, *"I am here to help you safeguard your memories."* Our words are so important. Our sensitivity and our emotional connection should be a big part of our fiber and directly affects how we approach our clients. These traits don't only help us procure listings; they help us work effectively with our clients through the entire sales process.

She made me a cup of tea, and as we packed each picture frame, she told me the story attached to it. She cried at the sight of her wedding picture. She cried when I packed the picture of her son playing by the pool. She told me stories of the vacations they took, the parties they had, and the day she lost her husband. My heart broke. I really wanted to tear up the listing contract and tell her to stay, but it was time. She knew it, the kids knew it, and so did I. More than anything, I wanted her to be able to just stay in her house and not need to sell it, but I knew it was time for her to leave and begin a new chapter in her life.

After packing, the house was de-cluttered. As she made some lunch, I went to my car and took out the cleaning supplies. I knew I could not do too much cleaning because it would offend her. I decided to tackle the most necessary areas and not worry about the rest. I started in the bathrooms. I scrubbed until the bleach entered my sinus cavity and gave me a headache for three days! LOL! I think I spent about three hours scrubbing and cleaning the bathrooms, kitchen, bedrooms and the front porch. When I was done, I knew the house was ready for public viewing.

On the day of the open house, I had her kids take her out to lunch, so she didn't have to witness people invading her home. One Open House and it was SOLD! The escrow closed in 15 days with a cash offer. My 90-year-old client moved out and passed away shortly after. I still drive by the house and remember her smile and her stories as I packed away her life. For me, it feels good knowing that I was able to work with her in that fragile, but very important time of her life.

I love my clients. I tell them that too. It has been my honor to serve them. I am more than a Realtor to them. I am their friend.

You cannot be upset with the world

when you keep getting

the same results

over and over

You're the one

who didn't do the work

Julie Sands

Let Me Say This

When you are a new Agent, it can be scary to talk to strangers. I know this because I used to be afraid to do it as well. I consider myself an outgoing person, but when it came to asking for business, I flunked. However, as a Top Producing Realtor, I talk to everyone now. I remember thinking to myself that every person I let pass by was missing out on my skill and expertise. If they only knew how passionate I was about real estate; if they only knew how much I would love to help them, if they only knew my staging and marketing skills; if they only knew how much I need to pay my car note and house note. LOL! So, I had to jump. I had to get over my fear of approaching total strangers and telling them about my services.

At any time, you need to be able to tell a potential client how you are going to make effective use of your services and convince them that you are better than the other Agents out there. You can help them move from feeling fear into a place of confidence. Let them know that you are able and willing to help them. Be committed to becoming the real estate professional that will walk them through this stage of their life and the one who is going to get their house sold for the price point that is the highest the market will bear. People are not looking for somebody who can just throw a sign out in front of their house and hope that someone will come in, make a full price offer and buy it. People need a professional presence, someone that can step in during this important phase of their life and lead the way.

All the phases of this process; decluttering the house, staging, making upgrades, putting a contract in place for the listing that protects both of you, working with the buyer to meet both the needs of the buyer and protect the needs of your seller, all result in the closing day. As they finalize the papers and see the proceeds from the sale of their house, your goal is to make them glad that they hired you. You want them to say, "*I am so glad that I met that real estate lady.*"

If you can do that and if you are really committed to being the Real Estate Agent who is an expert professional in the neighborhood that you are going to farm; if you put in the work, the hours, and commit yourself to the learning process, you will begin to find yourself making more and more money in real estate.

And Finally

Listen, I have been in the real estate industry for 30 years. I have loved every minute. (Well, most minutes. LOL!) I have been chased by dogs, followed, kicked out, ignored, told off, hung up on, and honked at. I have showed property in the rain, and I have been rained on. I have had my fair share of quick fast food lunches and dirty cars. I've been up to my ears in paperwork and I've had many late-night blues. Would I change it? Never!

I have also met the greatest people. I have been loved, appreciated, cared for, spoiled, respected, welcomed and made to feel like a superstar in the lives of my clients. I am blessed to have their trust, and I do not take that lightly, nor do I take it for granted. I know I am well respected in my industry. That was my intention, and I worked hard for that.

I would absolutely be honored and delighted to help you learn all these skills. I have a coaching program that I have developed especially for you, to take you from where you are now to become the real estate expert that is well on her way to getting rich. I look forward to working with you. I want to hear your stories, your successes, and even help you through your struggles. Together, we are going to help you build a real estate career.

Julie Sands is available for guest appearances, television guest, radio, podcast, seminars, conferences and speaking engagements.

You may also contact Julie for personal and business coaching programs.

For more information or to contact Julie Sands, you may use the following:

www.JulieSands.com
www.Facebook.com/itsjuliesands
www.Instagram.com/itsjuliesands
www.twitter.com/itsjuliesands

"For God so loved the world that he gave his one and only Son, that whoever believes in him shall not perish but have eternal life."
John 3:16